THE POWER OF READING

Great Ways to Build Good Habits, Acquire Knowledge, Develop Growth Mindset, and Achieve Long Term Success in Life.

PRADIP N DAS

Table of Content

Table of Content...2

How Can This Book Transform Your Life?.................3

Introduction 4

Why Do People Not Read?.................................. 16

Reading Improves Focus 23

Reading Improves Creativity 29

Reading Builds Character...................................... 37

Reading Improves Imagination 46

Reading Improves Knowledge................................. 53

Reading Improves Memory.................................... 64

Reading Improves Analytical Skills 73

Reading Improves Languages................................. 83

Reading Improves Writing 93

Reading Reduces Stress 102

How To Improve Reading 110

Book Summary 116

Disclaimer 121

COPYRIGHT © 2021 PRADIP N DAS...................... 122

Gratitude.................. **Error! Bookmark not defined.**

How Can This Book Transform Your Life?

After publishing a series of books on different elements of success, I decided to deviate slightly from my usual topic and write a book on one of the most important habits which every person should have. The book "The Power of Reading" is an effort to highlight several benefits of reading books in a very simple way and has covered methods to improve your reading as well. I am confident that this book will ignite your passion for reading books in you. It will create a habit which many people aspire to have.

You have made an awesome choice to transform your life by reading this book. Thank you very much, and I wish you all the best in building the habit of reading books and success in life.

"Reading is a superpower that helps to rule the world" - Bill gates.

Imagine what your life would be like if you read one book a week for the next 10 years of your life. Can you imagine the impact reading will have on your life? Do you believe that your knowledge, skills, mindset, focus, imagination, creativity will increase with reading?

Books are very powerful; they change and transform lives. Nearly all successful people will tell you that there is at least one that completely turned around and transformed their life.

But reading is not just about gathering information; it is coming together of many things. Reading can bring you great enjoyment and laughter, which is great for your well-being, while mystery novels will stimulate your imagination.

Reading can help you with loneliness or boredom; reading is ideal for passing the time away, especially during commutation.

Books are powerful ways of influencing the subconscious mind. You cannot succeed in life with limited knowledge and information.

Successful People and Leaders Read

If you look at top most people of the world, most of them have a habit of reading. Once Warren Buffett was asked about his secret to success, he simply pointed to a stack of books and said, *"Read 500 pages like this every day. That's how knowledge works. It builds up like compound interest. All of you can do it, but I guarantee not many of you will."* In his early career, Buffett would read 800 pages a day, not 500. Even now, he still reads for about 8 hours a day.

In an interview with The New York Times, Bill Gates shared that he reads about 50 books a year. He usually takes reading vacations for two weeks at a time.

Elon Musk, the founder of Tesla, SpaceX, and a serial technology entrepreneur, reads at least 500 pages a day. Long before he became the CEO of Tesla, and even before he cofounded PayPal, a young Elon Musk used to read science fiction novels for up to 10 hours a day. He read the entire Encyclopedia Britannica when he was 9 years old. Elon Musk has said that he taught himself physics and rocket science simply by reading a lot of books.

Oprah Winfrey has referred to reading as her "path to personal freedom." She selects one of her favorite books every month for her Book Club members to read and discuss. Mark Cuban spends up to about 3 hours of his day reading.

Mark Zuckerberg, the founder and the CEO of Facebook, swears to read one book every week. *"Books allow you to fully explore a topic and immerse yourself in a deeper way than most media today. I am looking forward to shifting more of my media diet towards reading books,"* he wrote in a Facebook post.

For the Best-Selling Author and Philanthropist Tony Robbins, reading books shaped his life for the better. In his words, *"I took a speed-reading course and read 700 books in seven years — all on psychology, physiology, anything that could make a difference in life."*

Jeff Bezos, founder and the CEO of Amazon, reads 3 hours per day. Even former US President Obama used to read a lot. All of them are self-declared voracious readers who take time out of their busy schedules to read, read and read.

Mahatma Gandhi was a voracious reader; he had read books almost on everything during his time spent in jail – related to Islam, Christianity, health hygiene, Hinduism, childbirth, Hindu philosophy, American prohibition, and many more. He was very much fond of reading books. His bookshelf was a list of classics he was very much fond of reading.

India's first Prime Minister, Pandit Jawaharlal Nehru, first woman Prime Minister Indira Gandhi, former Prime Minister Shri. PV Narasimha Rao and Shri. Atal Bihari Vajpayee, present Prime Minister Shri. Narendra Modi, former President Abdul Kalam Azad, and former President Pranav Mukherjee are examples in Indian history who were avid readers of books.

These famous people and almost every successful people love to read because they understand the importance of learning and improving. They understand the value of knowledge and how it can help them grow and move ahead in this life.

You should start reading books, particularly self-help books, which will help you learn a different perspective of life and helps you to learn and improve towards the betterment of yourself and the betterment of this world.

Importance of Reading Books

Reading is important because it matures our thoughts, gives us endless knowledge and lessons while keeping our minds active. Books can hold and keep all kinds of information, stories, thoughts, and feelings unlike anything else in this world. The importance of a book to help us learn and understand things cannot be underestimated.

In fact, for years, reading was the only form of personal entertainment, and perhaps this is why reading has been in the spotlight for such a long time. Reading has survived the years, and luckily, the benefits have survived right along with the books. So, let's talk about some reasons why reading is so important.

Reading as a Habit

Reading is a very good habit that one needs to develop in life. Good books are resourceful, give you knowledge, enlighten you with wisdom, and lead you in the right direction. There is no better companion than a good book. Reading is important because it is good for your overall well-being. Once you start developing reading habits, you experience a whole new world. Reading develops language skills and vocabulary. Reading books is also a way to relax and reduce stress. It is important to read a good book for a few minutes each day to stretch the brain muscles for healthy functioning.

This is something that all highly successful people know — that if they can get the right book in their hands, then the rest will naturally flow their way.

The habit of reading is one of the best qualities one can possess. Books are known to be your best friend for a reason. Reading helps build your confidence, reduces your stress, and puts you in a good mood. Once you start reading and make it your habit, you will eventually get addicted to it.

Reading is a very good habit that one needs to develop in life. Good books can inform you, enlighten you and lead you in the right direction. There is no better companion than a good book. Reading is important because it is good for your overall well-being. Once you start reading, you experience a whole new world. When you start loving the habit of reading, you eventually get addicted to it. Reading develops language skills and vocabulary. Reading books is also a way to relax and reduce stress. It is important to read a good book for a few minutes each day to stretch the brain muscles for healthy functioning.

Benefits of Books

We perform certain activities because of benefits. If a gym is for a healthy and fit body, reading can be considered a brain gym. If you are a person who is not fond of reading, then you might be missing out. People often don't understand the Benefits of Reading Books. Reading is a good habit as it gives several benefits. By reading books, we can feel the company of subject experts. Through newspapers, we get to know what is happening around us. Regular reading of an article or book has benefits. It may be gaining knowledge, passing an examination, getting a job, or developing an interesting hobby. Such benefits are motivators for study. Many great people have put their whole life experience in Autobiographies, or some people have written about the life of other great personalities in Biographies. By reading these, one can get motivated. Further, books are cheap, and hence, reading them is the cheapest method that one can easily afford compared to hiring a teacher or mentor for the same subject. However, it may not improve the extent that can be easily attained by mentoring by the same person.

Though reading might seem like simple fun, it can be helping your body and mind without you even realizing what is happening. Reading can be more important for these reasons and not just knowledge. For those who don't enjoy reading, you might change your mind after hearing about the benefits. Reading can greatly benefit you in many different ways—such as sharpening your mind, imagination, and writing skills. With so many advantages of reading, it should be an everyday occurrence to read at least a little something.

Yes, when we read biographies, we know the different people in our life without meeting them. If you read about the biography of Einstein, you will know the struggle and joy in his life, his success, his sacrifices for success in life.

Life is short; you cannot experience all things in life on your own and implement them in your life. Because of that, if you want to be more successful in your life, you have to know pits and falls and how to handle them.

Books are your best friends as you can rely on them when you are bored, upset, depressed, lonely, or annoyed. They will accompany you anytime you want them and enhance your mood. They share with you the information and knowledge you need. Good books always guide you to the correct path in life.

Reading is Like Investing in Yourself

Have you heard of the word ROI, i.e., Return on Investment, and have maximum ROI when you invest in yourself, and one of the best ways of investing in yourself is READING.

Books are like mentors and guides. Have you ever wondered or thought about the importance of a mentor or guide in one life? If yes, then books are the best mentor till you do not find a person as a mentor. Even after finding that person, reading will guide you in another field of knowledge.

To create the best version of yourself, you should read every day. Books rewire our brains in a new direction. Reading books eliminate distractions from our mind and give our mind a proper direction. It also increases our imagination power.

Let's understand all the benefits of reading in this book, which will help you get a proper direction for future action.

Why Do People Not Read?

After the advent of television in 1927, the reading of books has gradually declined over the years. Television has the potential to generate both positive and negative effects. It has made an immense contribution to our education and knowledge. But it has many negative effects, too, particularly deplete the capacity of critical thinking. Compared to reading a book, you can pause after reading a sentence to understand its true meaning; TV does not work that way. You receive the information; there is no time to analyze the information.

When somebody watches television, it is easier to feed meaningless information into people's minds than with books because it requires more effort to learn from reading a book. In the 1980s and 1990s, people became addicted to their TVs and slowly pushed their books aside. Then came the cable TV, which runs 24 x 7.

Therefore, attention span was dropping over the years and drastically over the last two decades. Many people lost the habit of reading long articles. They no longer have the patience and persistence required to comprehend complex write-ups. Now people have access to computers, the Internet, Games, Smartphones, and Tablets, Social media such as Facebook, Twitter, Instagram, WhatsApp, etc. These are the super distractors that keep people away from books - even academic books.

To read is difficult, or, more accurately, wanting to read can be difficult. There are a hundred reasons why people may not often read, if at all.

Some people find reading difficult, tedious, or boring. They'd rather do other physical activities or explore other media. I have found a number of these people are visually oriented and prefer getting the story through the action and visuals of a movie/video to reading the book itself.

Some people are resistant to reading because reading seems to be a punishment rather than a pleasure throughout their life. Following are the common reasons why people do not read books: -

1. No time to read

    Certainly, life gets in the way of a lot of things. People have different priorities in life and engage in many other activities. People are unable to give priority to reading over other things in life.

2. Difficult to decide what to read

There is a galaxy of books on each topic. Every year, millions of books are published in the USA alone. There are so many different genres and authors. So, is it difficult for somebody to decide what to read?

3. Reading is hard

Reading is not easy, particularly for those who are not habituated to reading. Some people find it very hard. People read books for many reasons, but you don't have to feel that it's an academic experience if you don't want it to be. Entertainment is one of the best reasons for reading. A book can incite unforgettable experiences, such as laugh, cry, excite, motivate, inspire.

4. Not habituated to read

Many people are not habituated to read. Sometimes, they are scared to see themselves in front of the book, hindering their start. It's not that difficult to make books and literature a part of your life. Start with something manageable and work your way up.

"I have a passion for teaching kids to become readers, to become comfortable with a book, not daunted. Books shouldn't be daunting, they should be funny, exciting and wonderful; and learning to be a reader gives a terrific advantage." – Roald Dahl.

5. Attention Span

Attention span is more as gratification is more immediate with other forms of media such as movies and video games. In a movie, the opening scene could be a volcano erupting to entice the viewer and keep them hooked. A similar scene could take several sentences to paragraphs to write in a book, depending on the author. Books are not the medium for people that want instant gratification.

6. Solo Activity

People like to watch movies and play video games with friends. Books are inherently a solo activity that is enjoyed alone. The most social activity you can do with a book is discussing it with friends after reading it.

7. Books Are Expensive

While it may be true that owning books was once considered a luxury, these days, there are numerous sources of inexpensive literature. The Internet has opened a whole new arena for readers. Literature, both old and new, is available on your phone for free or at steeply discounted prices.

8. Total Commitment

Reading a book requires much commitment as the person needs to sit down and actually read it. Unlike TV, you can't have dinner or chitchat with people while reading. Your eyes have to be focused, and your hands occupied. Some people, especially inexperienced readers, have trouble concentrating when there is background noise too.

Reading Improves Focus

Focus is the key to success. Focus involves the ability to pay attention to things that help and avoid all distractions. The more you are focused on the subject or task, the more you go deep into the subject. Focus brings attention, creates ideas, and increases productivity.

Focus is very important because it is the gateway to all our thought processes, such as learning, reasoning, problem solving, perception, memory, and decision making. Without focus, you will not be able to concentrate on the right things; you will not be getting your work done productively.

The mind can effectively work when you focus on a single activity at a time. By focusing on one thing at a time, you can concentrate deeply on the task, think more creatively about the solution, and complete it faster than usual. It increases productivity and brings better results much more quickly than multitasking. The more focused you are, the more productive and fruitful your work will be.

Impact of Reading in Focus

In today's internet world, attention shifts very fast in other directions, and people keep multitasking every day. But when you read a book, all your attention is on the story, and all the world is far away, and you can immerse yourself in every fine detail you are absorbing. So, when you read, you focus on content and learn to ignore outside factors. Reading habits make your mind in a tranquil state. For many, reading is like meditation.

There is nothing better than spending leisure time at weekends relaxing with your head buried in a book where you can calm your mind, so make books your loyal friend and companion. You get better at focusing on things, analyzing things, and extracting the important stuff out of things. You tend to be more passionate, which begins to reflect in your writings, and you get better at another talent.

While you are reading, your mind concentrates on only one activity, i.e., reading, which helps you increase your focus and concentration. Reading also helps improve memory; after reading an article, try recalling it after some time. Trying to recall is like an exercise for your mind.

Reading a book is a great way of taking your focus out of everyday troubles and concerns; it takes you to seemingly better places of dreamlike and fantasy worlds for a while. The mind is like the body; it needs exercise just like your muscles do. This can soon begin to help you relax your mind and body and give you some much-needed rest which can help you energize yourself. You build on your concentration since it becomes essential to understand the complete flow and connect with the story/content as a whole.

How Reading Improve Focus and Concentration

Reading helps improve concentration. Reading can train our mind on how to focus properly, which is invaluable in nearly everything we do daily, whether as we study or even in our careers and personal relationships. We could all benefit from practicing our concentration skills.

Reading takes us out of that 'multi-tasking' mindset that we are constantly in. It allows us to really focus on one thing that we are doing and for a long time. This focus can allow us to succeed in other parts of our lives, such as on the job. Those who can focus for longer periods can get more work done and be more efficient, which can mean working fewer overall hours or being seen as a more valuable worker.

Reading improves our concentration and improves our attention span, focus, and improves our brain connectivity. If you are struggling to concentrate or focus, you can try reading as it is one of the best methods to improve concentration. Reading puts our brain to work and offers a deeper view of ideas, concepts, emotions, and body of knowledge. Reading involves several brain functions, including visual and auditory processes and many more.

Especially when we are reading something fictional like any of the novel, all of our attention is focused on the story or gaining a better understanding of a particular topic— the rest of the world just falls away, and we can immerse ourselves in every fine detail we're absorbing.

Reading is a good hobby to engage in for all age groups. It helps slow down the cognitive decline in older people. Reading is useful for a child as it helps him/her learn, build their vocabulary, connect and relate, develop new language and communicate better. It is beneficial for adults to engage in reading as it relieves stress and improves one's memory.

Reading Improves Creativity

'There was a mighty King who lived in a luxurious palace mounted at the top of a mountain. The King had a mighty army of around 20000 soldiers protecting the fort.....'.

I am sure while reading this fictitious story; you had vivid pictures created in your mind. As it has been said, imagination is a tool for creativity. We can only read when we imagine the things being written. This is how reading makes you imaginative, leading to creativity.

Our Brain is Like a Computer Processor

Our brain is like a super-powerful advanced computer, and like all good computers, the better the information in, the better the information out. Like all good computers, your mind needs good information for good output. Reading is the best source of inputs you can feed the brain.

You need to nourish your brain with new and good information. Without new information mind become stagnant. Reading feeds your hungry mind with an endless supply of knowledge and information which it seeks. Reading can help broaden your mind or keep you intrigued in a storyline where the power of curiosity will make you want to get to the end of the book as quickly as possible.

Reading and Creative Thinkers

Reading increases your imagination and creativity. It also gives you different ideas and understanding. A good reader from a young age can become a good writer. Reading sparks ones' imagination. When you read, you are taken into the new world. The content nurtures your brain to develop ideas for new worlds and other possibilities, which sparks the imagination. Reading helps you to understand differently.

Reading exposes you to the world of imagination; it shows you nothing is impossible in this world, shows how different actions lead to different results. Books help you to change your fixed mindset to a growth mindset.

Research says that the brain requires exercise to keep it strong and healthy. Hence reading can be the best exercise to keep your brain healthy, fit, and strong. Similarly, games like Chess, puzzle, analytical reasoning, etc., can also stimulate the brain.

Great books have been written by some of the best and most creative minds. By reading those books, you can delve into what goes on in the inner world of the great thinkers, and accordingly, you can expand and develop your own mind and knowledge.

Reading can, for a pleasant while, take you away from normality. Reading a fiction book gives you a chance to enter a fantasy, suspense, and curiosity domain just by engaging your attention. Reading self-help books can enrich your mind with advice, solutions, direction, inspiration, etc. It will expand your awareness and knowledge; each book or article will make you wiser and more intelligent.

Life becomes so much more interesting when you explore new avenues or venture into somebody else's imagination and creativity. Because books are small and compact, you can take a book with you anywhere you go, and they need no power supply, no charging of the battery, no interruption in between unless you do.

Reading is one of the cheapest forms of entertainment. It can stimulate your analytical thinking abilities and skills. It is even freely available on the internet or in libraries.

Reading Stimulates Your Creativity

Not many people have achieved success without knowledge and learning; the best way to absorb and acquire knowledge is through reading. One of the most powerful yet probably underestimated personal development tools is reading.

The benefits of reading are limitless, and it is an age-old tradition and past time which will never become dated. With the technological revolution forever gathering pace, many people now overlook the many health and therapeutic benefits of reading. Reading takes you to the world of imagination and enhances your creativity. Reading helps you explore life from different perspectives. While you read books, you are building new and creative thoughts, images, and opinions in your mind. It makes you think creatively, fantasize and use your imagination.

Many people like to grab a book, find a cozy corner and forget all their cares and worries for a while as they experience and enjoy the peace and tranquility gained by switching off and forgetting about the rest of the world. You can never be alone if you are reading.

Words describing scenes can never be entertaining if you cannot imagine what they are trying to depict. To be able to enjoy a book truly, your mind is forced to imagine the scenes, and a compelling book is capable enough to turn your imagination into a movie of sorts, running just for you, in your mind.

Our brains are never wired to work a particular way. We make it happen through our actions. Reading fiction books stimulates our creative thinking. We come up with different scenarios, alternate endings, and our own interpretations. This slowly improves our creativity.

Another one of the many reasons why reading is important is that it allows for creative thinking. Reading can inspire you when you are feeling bored, down, or in a rut. It can help give you that very needed pick-me-up without having to search too far for it. Reading helps get the creative side of your brain thinking, unlike television that really does not use much creative brainpower.

How to Develop Creativity

Successful people read with the purpose of improving their understanding of the world. Creativity requires fuel, and that fuel includes gaining knowledge through reading and studying new things. The best innovators are the biggest learners and not just limited to the fields directly related to their work. They are the first readers; they know they can't maintain the leading edge while waiting for inspiration to strike. Reading stimulates imagination which leads to the development of correlation which further develops creativity. It does not stop here; it then develops problem-solving skills.

So for every book, look for one main idea that you find new, useful, or challenges your existing beliefs. For example, when we see a movie, we can describe the main plot after months, but we don't care to register the paint color of the hero's office. If you try to remember the whole book, it will take away the joy. You need to learn "one big thing" from each book, and you will be on your way to success.

Reading Builds Character

"Knowing others is intellect, Knowing yourself is true wisdom. Mastering others is courage, Mastering yourself is true power".
- M. Nasreen

Character is a set of beliefs that describe what kind of person you are. It shows your way of dealing with people, achieving your goals, obeying your habits, discipline, thought process, etc. Your opinion of another person's character is based on the impression the person makes concerning his or her attitudes or actions toward things you value.

What You Read, You Become

People read books in many different ways. A book may contain wisdom, but it doesn't necessarily translate to the reader, so it important to read, recognize, research, and discuss to garner wisdom unless you already have the knack of doing that.

Books are a way of incorporating other people's experiences, not necessarily limited to those who live but those who died centuries ago. Reading takes the reader to a different world and shows the world through the eyes of various characters. Reading can rewire the human mind.

What you read has a direct impact on your mind and, therefore, on your personality. Researchers found that Reading books allow you to see things from the perspective of the author. Books give you new ideas. You are constantly learning when you are reading, and you can start to look at the world from a more balanced perspective. Otherwise, you tend to think in one direction based on your past in the absence of other viewpoints. It improves your power of understanding others and thinking patterns.

Generally, people who regularly read fiction books are more friendly, sympathetic, and well-behaved towards others. People who spend more time watching television, using social media on the phone or laptop than reading is more likely to be arrogant and less sociable.

How Reading Develops Character

Reading is paramount in developing yourself. It gives you access to the thoughts of wise people who lived before your time.

A person made most of the mistakes you made and are going to make at some time. Fortunately, some of those mistakes were documented. So, reading will definitely help you to understand the mistakes already made by others and to tackle such problems.

But the reason you should read great books is that they challenge your beliefs, they question your character. It is an incredibly difficult thing for a person to challenge themselves, as it means you are invalidating a part of your identity. Eventually, if you are open-minded enough, you will start to see the point made by the other side. You will begin to understand that the world is not black and white. It is much greyer than you think. This is process of building character. And that's why it is called BUILDING the character.

When you realize that maybe you are wrong, you search for other options. This process expands your mind to absorb the views and beliefs of other people. You start to understand their perspective. Books enable this attitude.

Reading good books shapes your personality, your way of thinking, and your observation power. You can realize the change in you. Every book you read has an impact on your personality.

Reading Makes You Smarter

Reading helps you to become better. When you are reading, you are training your brain, and reading gives wisdom to your mind. Reading helps you to understand yourself. Differently. It opens up your mind, helps you accept the changes in your life, makes you understand the different positive aspects of life, and helps you understand the world more properly. Knowledge is the key to success, and hence having knowledge about life about different things will help you move ahead in life and make your brain sharper and make you smarter.

Reading Helps You To Grow

The benefits of reading are enormous; some books will inspire you. Reading inspirational stories or reading where people have already achieved what you aim to achieve can give you the motivation you need.

Reading is significant, everybody who wants to better their life should read more, because when you stop learning you stop growing. There is an abundance of knowledge and information available in the form of books because the more you read, the wiser you will become and the more you will grow.

Reading can make you travel through a different world. When reading, you forget your own world and move into a world created by the author. You let your mind wander into worlds where no man has gone. You begin to interact with ideas and characters at the subconscious level.

When most people try and relax normally, they find it hard to switch off their racing minds. Sometimes it can be difficult for some people to shut off their thoughts simply.

Therefore, Reading helps you shape your character to a great extent, boosting your confidence and personality.

Reading Makes You Intelligent

Books are your best friend. They are a powerhouse of knowledge and wisdom. Books have so much to give us, and do not expect anything in return. A good book can uplift one's mood instantly and leave a deep impact on us. It is prudent to read different kinds of books to grow wiser. Books develop one's personality in a better way. Reading helps in arranging your thoughts and helps you express yourself better. Your way of expressing yourself become clearer.

Reading helps you to become intelligent. Reading increases your intellect and improves your concentration, thus making you a wiser and interesting person. Books allow you to see things from a completely different perspective. For example, reading a book about a certain value or habit can help you to understand how that value or habit differs from your own. You might not agree with that perspective, but at least you will look at things from a new angle.

With reading, it is obvious that you can gain more self-confidence and express yourself fluently in both written and verbal. Reading gives you a broad knowledge of everything and everyone surrounding you. It helps you recognize that not everyone has the same psychological attitude that you do. When you learn to empathize with the characters in a book, you learn to realize people in real life as well. While reading, you need to remember the minute specifics about the characters. Hence, this helps in remembering and recalling the characters when needed in the trick of the story. And believe it, this is the most important factor.

Books help a lot in improving your own performance and way of thinking. When you start reading and analyzing things, your focus and concentration automatically increase. It gives you inner peace. In the process of getting enduring to reading, you start connecting with yourself and reading what you like instead of what you love. This commonly brings a sort of calmness and inner peace to you. This helps in lowering your blood pressure levels and also keeps your mood swings. Reading uplifts your knowledge and makes better use of your time. You can also start to connect with new people and make new friends. You get into networking and get connected with people of identical interests. Reading books can help make you a better person in every way.

Reading Improves Imagination

"Imagination is more important than knowledge. For while knowledge defines all we currently know and understand, imagination points to all we might yet discover and create" - Albert Einstein

The imagination is a powerful tool that can be useful in all aspects of life. Though it might not be considered often, imagination allows us to be empathetic with people. This empathy can help on the job or even at home. Reading is an excellent way to improve your imagination; it is no wonder that books have been a favorite for so many years.

Although the enhancement of your imagination is not one of the more common benefits, reading can significantly increase your imagination. Consider the worlds that you are immersed in and the characters you come across while reading a novel. Because of them, the part of your brain which houses your imagination is stimulated, causing you to imagine what the places and people look like just by picturing the words.

When you begin reading a book, you usually don't have a picture in your head right at the start. By the time you finish the book, you can easily imagine the entire world and characters filling the book. Reading books is all due to the stimulation of the brain that reading induces. Voracious readers will know the feeling of losing themselves in the worlds of novels. It is a wonderful feeling.

Reading is a beautiful escape from the nuances of the mundane world. You can sit comfortably on your couch and yet get transported into a different world altogether—a world with so many possibilities, opinions, and mysteries. The best part about reading is that it leaves so much to your imagination as you create pictures in your mind through words. And these pictures create an experience that is all yours, hidden in the depths of your mind.

Reading Engages Your Imagination

Storybooks can engage you in a world that is miles apart from our own; here, you can have a glimpse of what goes on in the lives of many fictional characters.

When you engage your curious mind in a book, you can experience empathy, sympathy, and compassion with these make-believe characters. This shows the power of your imagination as you bring these people and their experiences to life.

You can travel anywhere through a book, and you get to meet and engage with the author and their fantasy worlds. Fiction books will allow you to use your imagination to paint your own version of the images, characters, and places.

Every book can give a different representation of the characters and the location to each reader because everybody's imagination will perceive things slightly differently.

Reading requires you to use your creative imagination; stories stimulate curiosity, intrigue you; books are the best way to stir your creativity and absorb knowledge.

In fact, reading has such a powerful influence; it can change your emotional state, sad stories can make you feel sad, stories of inspiration can motivate and inspire you, while happy stories can improve our mood.

Reading can significantly increase your imagination. When you start reading, you come across a word, character, or place, and then you try to imagine how it looks, which enhances your imagination power.

The more we read, the better we can build up and expand our knowledge. We can be open to new ideas and have an understanding of new things. Reading helps us practice imagination by letting the words describe a certain image while the reader manipulates the picture in mind. This practice strengthens the mind as it acts like a muscle. But what are the benefits of imagination?

Famous physicist Albert Einstein thought imagination was more important than knowledge because someone with a good imagination could find new discoveries and create. Scientists and educationists now know that reading can broaden the imagination by stimulating the right side of the brain, literally opening up a person's mind to new ideas and possibilities.

Benefits of Imagination

Imagination has many benefits. It encourages creativity, which brings about new ideas. It also plays a huge part in innovation. Without imagination, people wouldn't be able to come up with new inventions and new ideas that help advance society. It also pushes discovery and understanding. Reading is a key part of enhancing imaginative thinking, which can lead to innovation and understanding.

The scientists also found that readers could forget mundane problems while totally focused on reading a novel and letting their imaginations soar. Brain networks can be reconfigured for days, and this may help shape a child's brain.

Reading broadens our imagination by stimulating the right side of our brain. It literally opens our minds to new possibilities and new ideas, helping us experience and analyze the world through others' lives.

It is found that reading a good novel allows one's imagination to take flight and allows you to forget about your day-to-day troubles. Reading a good science fiction novel, for example, can transport you to a fantasy world that becomes a reality in your mind's eye.

Lead Emory researcher Gregory Berns concluded, "At a minimum, we can say that reading stories—especially those with strong narrative arcs—reconfigures brain networks for at least a few days. It shows how stories can stay with us. This may have profound implications for children and the role of reading in shaping their brains."

Reading Improves Knowledge

"Reading is important because if you can read, you can learn anything about everything and everything about anything."
– Tomie dePaola

Can books really open your mind, expand your knowledge, and transform the way you live? Nothing else can expand your knowledge as much as book reading can do. I cannot say whether reading a book will expand your knowledge as much as reading anything else. Books have expanded my knowledge a great deal and opened my mind. Indeed, books show me to solve many problems in life and uncover new interests. They have helped me excel in life and my career. Above all else, books have brought me closer to a meaningful and effective way of leading life.

Consider this situation. You plant a seed. You water them daily. You make sure that it gets all the things essential for its growth. Finally, it sprouts. After a long time, it grows to become a big tree. It now has branches and leaves, and it provides fruits and shade for others and helps them survive!

Similarly, we should consider the seed as 'our mind' and the water and other things we add as 'knowledge.' We see a whole new world of knowledge in front of us. This knowledge can not only become beneficial to us but the whole world.

Reading is one of the primary ways to acquire knowledge. The knowledge you gain is cumulative and grows exponentially. When you have a strong knowledge base, it's easier to learn new things and solve new problems. Reading a wide range of books will help expand your general knowledge. Specific knowledge can be acquired by taking a deep dive into a subject or topic. Filling your mind with new facts, new information, and new ideas will make you a better conversationalist as you'll always have something interesting to talk about.

Impact of Reading

The more we read books, the more we develop ourselves in the light of knowledge. The light of knowledge increases the power of our minds and expands its scope. Reading broadens our imagination by stimulating the right side of our brain. It literally opens our minds to new possibilities and new ideas, helping us experience and analyze the world through others' lives.

So, all the great and wise men of the world always read and encouraged reading books because we discover new horizons of life by reading. We know ourselves deeply, understand the world in the real context and find meaning in life just by reading books. If you can enjoy reading books and turn them into a habit, your perception of life may change.

The major impact of reading is that along with knowledge; we can also acquire wisdom and intelligence that expands our imagination power. If you can gain more advanced imagination power, the more creative you would be, and the more successful you will be in life.

The More You Read, The More You Know

Regardless of the type of the book, each book gives you something to learn, be it only the opinion of an individual (the author) alone, maybe. It teaches you about how people think and act, about various places, about science, philosophy, and much more. It makes you ask questions that you could never have thought about without that book. This knowledge broadens your mind and makes you more accepting of people and situations. It also makes you prepared, if you have read about it, for situations that you have never encountered in life. Everything you read fills your head with new bits of information, and you never know when it might come in handy. The more knowledge you have, the better equipped you are to tackle any challenge you'll face.

The religious books from different religions are probably the earliest books ever written; they are like our guide and rule book of life with many hidden messages and words of guidance written in them for us to follow and adhere to.

One of the biggest advantages of reading, especially with the explosion of the internet, is that you gather information as you keep on learning. These days, information can make you money through websites and blogging.

How Does Reading Help You Gain Knowledge?

Every time you read, you know about different facts. You gain knowledge. You do understand the subject. And to know about these facts and to get information is to gain knowledge which is happening through reading.

Suppose you are reading the book "Seven Habits of Highly Effective People" by Stephen Covey. Now, what knowledge will you gain by reading the book, and how will it be acquired. When you read the book, you learn about the various powerful lessons described in this book. For instance, you will know how to deal with change and uncertainty, pro-activeness, think to win/win, put first things first, etc. As you read the book, you will be able to understand many such life-changing lessons. Your knowledge will increase as you understand the facts described in the book.

In fact, reading has many incredible benefits, and there are many reasons why we should develop a reading habit. Besides, reading helping you acquire knowledge, keeps your brain active and engaged, helps reduce stress, and expands your vocabulary.

Suppose you are reading a book about being a good writer, for example, Writer's Process by Anne Janzer. By reading this book, you will acquire some knowledge and skills related to the writing process.

Assuming you are a Marketing student and need to understand the various theories of marketing. You have heard lectures on it from your teacher, but you should read the various books on marketing by Philip Kotler if you want to go deeper.

Caution!!!

Although the benefits of reading are priceless, it is important to realize that reading can be very damaging and self-destructive if you absorb and believe negative opinions and destructive information.

So, avoid reading all negative, wrong, or unhelpful information or misleading, damaging suggestions; it can shatter your dreams and ambitions. It can dishearten you and fill you with negative and limiting beliefs. So, any information you feel is not helpful, reject it immediately and stop reading it.

An Effective Way of Gaining Knowledge by Reading Books

It is clear that people gain knowledge by reading books. You can use some effective methods to gain accurate and expected knowledge by reading books.

Henceforth, you will read the book with full attention and precisely understand what the author means when you read books. If you do not understand a part or line of a book, read that part again.

You can use highlighters to keep in mind very important words and ideas. You can discuss any important ideas with friends.

If, after reading a book, you will share the learning of the book with your friend, then the ideas will last long in you.

You can keep a diary with you while reading a book. Keep notes in your own language of the key ideas and technical term in the book that you think is crucial.

You can make a book reading schedule, read regularly, and read some books a second time if you feel the need.

By following all these things, you will surely gain maximum knowledge by reading books.

Finally, there is no denying that reading books add knowledge and imparts educations since childhood days. Be it fiction or nonfiction; you get to look a lot from books. It exposes you to the outer world, which helps you to acquire sensibility about worldly topics. Everything you read fills your head with new bits of information, and you never know when it might come further in your life. The more knowledge you have, the better-equipped you are to tackle any challenge you'll ever face. Throughout history, all sources of knowledge have been documented entirely in some form of readable text that is just sitting out there, waiting to be read. If you're curious and your thirst for knowledge is unquenchable, reading is what you should be doing. Books vest you with knowledge and wisdom. The grip on knowledge and book-reading go hand in hand. The oftener you read the books, the more you are studying real-life scenarios, and the more sophisticated you are. No one can beat an experienced and intelligent man. You are all set to succeed in your life.

"Reading brings knowledge and knowledge is power; therefore, reading is power. The power to know and learn and understand . . . but also the power to dream. Stories inspire us to reach high, love deep, change the world, and be more than we ever thought we could. Every book allows us to dream a new dream." – Emma Chase

"Reading is to the mind what exercise is to the body." - Joseph Addison

Our mind is an amazing thing, which can remember a lot of things with relative ease. But we usually do not use our brain as per the capability; we just fill our brain with all kinds of unwanted information and negativity that stop our brain's growth, resulting in a fixed mindset. Our mind has enormous capabilities; it just needs a workout just like our body to give its best performance.

How Reading Improves Memory?

1. Reading energizes the brain

Reading heightens brain alertness. Knowledge is food for the brain, and reading is like a workout for the brain. The more you read, the more you work out, the more your brain grows muscles.

This is a continuous learning process, and reading keeps your brain focused on this process. Many people like to read for pleasure which is always a plus point.

Like any muscle in your body, the brain needs exercise to keep it supple and healthy. The comparison of reading a book to a workout is not a new discovery.

2. Reading books strengthen memory

A mentally stable person can face challenging conditions at greater ease. You never lose your temperament as quickly as the ignorant. You are all set to handle the matters persuasively.

Reading at least a little each day stimulates the brain, particularly the part of the brain that helps with memory and attention. Like physical exercise, reading is a form of mental exercise that pushes your memory and focus to the limits. Simple reading comprehension improves your memory function. Because the part of the brain that controls memory is stimulated, it acts as an exercise for this part of the brain, resulting in improved memory.

Reading also improves your memory because each time a new idea pops from a book, you think about it, new synapses are formed. If you recognize something that is already stored in your brain, the old pathway will be strengthened, thus improving short-term memory.

It is shown that the habit of reading improves memory. When we read, we make the brain get used to remembering characters, facts, details, or situations, becoming a great mental exercise.

If you are looking for ways to improve your memory and concentration and also relieve stress, reading will help. The brain-stimulating activities from reading have been shown to slow down cognitive decline in old age with people who participated in more mentally stimulating activities over their lifetimes. It also has shown a slower rate of decline in memory and other mental capacities.

3. Reading improves focus

How does your focus improve through reading? Your focus is strengthened through reading because it requires focus to read. When sitting down to read a book or article, you will not understand what you are reading unless you're focused. Consider what it is like when doing a math problem. To get it correct, you have to focus intently on that problem. The same goes for reading. Again, like the memory function in your brain, your focus is exercised, which helps to improve your overall focus.

In the Stanford research, it is found that when you read, blood flows into brain regions associated with paying close attention to the task, confirming that reading improves your focus and concentration.

This is where the benefits of reading come into play, you can get that much-needed rest, and you can keep the mind occupied at the same time.

The beauty of this is you get your relaxation, and you can learn at the same time. This will keep the mind nourished and enriched, and it will improve your memory and concentration at the same time so you cannot lose.

Life-enhancing as these benefits of reading is, it seems that very few are aware or are purposefully in pursuit of them. From research by Pew Research Centre, only 3% said they like to be mentally challenged by (reading) books. The bulk of participants said they read to learn, gain knowledge, discover information, escape reality, immerse in another world, use their imagination, be entertained, find spiritual enrichment (close), and expand their worldview; about 2%, like the smell, feel and smell of physical books.

The 12% who said they enjoyed being relaxed while reading and having a quiet time was close to identifying a significant health benefit from reading.

Cognitive neuropsychologist Dr. David Lewis claimed that reading reduces stress by 68% whilst listening to music by 61%, having a cup of coffee or tea by 54%, and taking a walk by 42%. He found that reading silently for six minutes can slow down the heart rate and ease muscle tension.

The next time you feel angst building, you will know what to do. Keep calm and carry on reading.

Of course, reading will make you a better writer. You will subconsciously adopt a style and the techniques that resonate with you. You will also improve your spelling as you grow your vocabulary. Mental Floss, a knowledge magazine, shared a finding that avid readers can improve their vocabulary and fact-based knowledge by 50%.

In that same article, Mental Floss reported that a team at Yale University found that a daily dose of reading, for just 30 minutes at a go, may lengthen your lifespan by as much as two years. This conclusion is distilled from a study of 3600 adults over the age of 50 for 12 years. [1]

Dr. Wade Fish, Director at Northcentral University's Graduate School, said, "Reading expands a person's appreciation toward other life experiences the reader is not personally experiencing, especially when reading topics that are not related to that reader's job or lifestyle."

---

[1] Source: https://medium.com/@stulim/how-reading-can-improve-your-brains-processing-speed-up-to-100x-faster-d4738714c4de

"Reading is a fundamental skill needed to function in society. Words - spoken and written - are the building blocks by which a child's mind grows. Reading is not only essential to a child's verbal and cognitive development, but it also teaches the child to listen, develop a new language, and communicate. Additionally, books open a child's imagination into discovering his or her world." "Reading is a fundamental skill needed to function in society. Words - spoken and written - are the building blocks by which a person's mind grows. Reading is not only essential to a child's verbal and cognitive development, but it also teaches the person to listen, develop a new language, and communicate. Additionally, books open a person's imagination to discovering his or her world.

Reading Improves Analytical Skills

Analytical skills are very important to find solutions to common problems and help make decisions for the next actions. Understanding problems and analyzing the situation for viable solutions is a key skill in every position, every level. Developing this ability can improve your work, help you achieve company goals, and eventually support your personal career goals.

In a world of fierce competition and dynamic markets, it is essential to understand data because data speaks a lot. Analytical skills are critical for budgeting, competitor analysis, customer feedback, campaign performance, financial status, strategic planning, and so on. If you want to get more output at work, then you need to master analytical thinking. Analytical thinking is a powerful skill that helps detect patterns, brainstorm, observe, interpret data, and make decisions based on the multiple factors and options available to you.

Analytical skills are the ability to solve both simple and complex problems using all information available. Analytical skills can include various skills, but they are necessary for critical thinking and adept problem-solving. Analytical skills allow you to find solutions to common problems and help in making decisions for the next actions. Understanding problems and analyzing the situation for viable solutions is a key skill in every position, every level. Developing this ability can improve your work, help you achieve company goals, and eventually support your personal career goals.

Suppose you want to get more output at work. In that case, you need to master analytical thinking that helps detect patterns, brainstorm, observe, interpret data, and make decisions based on the multiple factors and options available to you.

Reading and Analytical Skills

Reading allows someone to constantly ask questions about the created world and find ways it parallels their own. Readers can discuss a book with another person and debate the symbolism and themes present in the novel. Even talking about your favorite character can build analytical skills! This is because it requires you to identify their various characteristics and relate why their personality may have resonated with you. You have to consider whether that character has a similar mindset to yours or if that character reminds you of someone you care about.

Books empower us and broaden the perspective of our thinking. They equip us with the knowledge of rational thought and analytical reasoning. The person with such qualities becomes a problem-solving giant.

Reading is great fun for many people, but it also has many benefits for your mental health in the form of thinking and understanding. By concentrating on the words and the storyline, it stimulates your brain and cognitive functions. This particular stimulation can help sharpen your mind, especially the part of the brain responsible for concentration and critical analysis. Reading sharpens this part of the brain much like you would sharpen a knife. This sharpening of the mind will eventually heighten your focus when concentrating on something important.

A good way to start improving your analytical skills is through the power of the written word. Reading stimulates your thinking and broadens your imagination. Reading boosts analytical thinking. Readers improve their general knowledge and can spot patterns quicker than non-readers. Indeed, the more you expose yourself to different ideas, the more you'll increase your cognitive abilities. Therefore, the key to improving your analytical thinking skills is to keep your mind active and running.

Reading Boost Critical Thinking

Critical thinking is an important skill to develop as a person grows. Good critical thinking skills can be attained in a variety of ways. Books that are best for creating critical thinkers are, surprisingly, fictional stories. Because fiction is more of an art form, readers must consider the inferences and symbolism within the story, which involves a much deeper level of thinking than nonfiction. They are involved in the detective process from beginning to end of each book, uncovering the mystery to collecting the clues, and coming to a solution at the end. This process of engaging readers adds to the value of these books when it comes to reading for critical thinking.

Thinking is something we do every day, often without being consciously aware of what we're doing. The thinking process requires prior knowledge, memory, and the use of that prior knowledge. Thinking can, in fact, be limited by a lack of experience and knowledge. The thinking process also requires language to organize and express thoughts.

Thinking requires experience, knowledge, and language to express thoughts, and reading is the process of constructing meaning and comprehension. The thinking ability is very important for middle school students to get more independent.

Learning to think about what you read is a central and most important part of the entire reading, comprehension, and learning process because, in every human communication, someone is trying to transmit his or her thinking.

By active reading, you explore several aspects of life. It involves questioning what you read. It helps you develop your thoughts and express your opinions. New ideas and thoughts pop up in your mind by active reading. It stimulates and develops your brain and gives you a new perspective.

Critical thinking skills are perhaps the most fundamental skills involved in making judgments and solving problems. You use them every day, and you can continue improving them.

The ability to think critically about a matter—to analyze a question, situation, or problem down to its most basic parts—is what helps us evaluate the accuracy and truthfulness of statements, claims, and information we read and hear. It is the sharp knife that, when honed, separates fact from fiction, honesty from lies, and the accurate from the misleading. We all use this skill to one degree or another almost every day.

How Does Reading Sharpen Your Mind?

It sharpens your mind through stimulation of the brain. By causing you to focus intensely on the words, your brain takes in a significant amount of information, which can improve both your critical thinking and analyzing skills as well. This stimulation is healthy for your mind and the sharpening your thought processes. Isn't it amazing how a book can do that? Of course, some of the most successful people in the world read every day, and they understand that knowledge is key. So, it may be time to heed their advice if you want to be closer to your dream.

Reading doesn't just help with your critical thinking, but it also improves your brain function. Consider what happens when you work a muscle every day. That muscle grows and becomes much stronger than before. Reading works much the same way for your mind. The constant stimulation of the brain that reading provides is similar to the exercise required to work a muscle; it strengthens the separate parts of the brain that control your thinking and analyzing skills.

A good way to start improving your analytical skills is through the power of the written word. Reading stimulates your thinking and broadens your imagination. Reading boosts analytical thinking. Readers improve their general knowledge and can spot patterns quicker than non-readers. Indeed, the more you expose yourself to different ideas, the more you'll increase your cognitive abilities. Therefore, the key to improving your analytical thinking skills is to keep your mind active and running.

Reading Improves Languages

Indian Parliamentarian and former UN Under-Secretary-General Shashi Tharoor's mastery over the English language is known to all. During an interaction with students at an event, a student asked Tharoor to give him a new word. In his response, Tharoor revealed how he developed his 'exotic' vocabulary. "I'll give you a very simple, old word – read – that's the only way I have acquired the vocabulary. People think I am some sort of nut case who studies dictionaries all day long...I have barely opened dictionary in my life," Tharoor said. The 63-year-old politician's response received huge applause from the audience. "I have read extensively...I had some advantages over all of you...I lived in India without television, without computers, without play station, without mobile phones... all I had were books," Tharoor added. [2]

Language is a vital part of human connection. Although all species have their ways of communicating, humans are the only ones that have mastered cognitive language communication. Language allows us to share our ideas, thoughts, and feelings with others. The many cognitive benefits of learning languages are undeniable.

Usage of the right words at the right spot wins you a lot of appreciation, credibility, and success. You can turn your worst enemy into a friend. By reading more and more books, you gather enough knowledge and vocabulary to express yourself better. It gives you a lot of

---

[2] Source: https://www.financialexpress.com/india-news/shashi-tharoor-secret-behind-his-vocabulary-tharoor-interaction-with-students-video-news/1766430/

confidence, and you can enjoy your status as an educated person in society.

Flair in Language

Being persuasive and well-spoken is of great help in any profession. Whether it is fiction or non-fiction, Shakespeare or Rick Riordan, you come to know about a lot regarding the language (or languages) and how it developed over time. You come to know about various colloquial sayings, the mannerisms, and the effect of the times on the characters' speech and are introduced to a vast array of words that, with time, get ingrained into your vocabulary. Thus, not only do you improve in that language, but you also get a perspective of people you encounter in real life, based on the way they use the language. The more you read, the more words you gain exposure to, and they will automatically make their way into your everyday vocabulary.

People often face problems related to language. But Reading can help you to improve, to learn new words, statements and grammar. Reading makes overall development in language, be it vocabulary, writing, or communication.

Reading Improves Your Quality of Conversations

Your vast array of new-found knowledge will help you to become more involved in discussions; you will be more able to instigate much more varied and interesting levels of conversations. Obtaining more information will give you a distinct advantage over the others because you will have gathered a much wider understanding of many subjects and topics of conversation. Limited knowledge can seriously hold you back and leave you feeling left out in some social situations.

Ultimately, this will make you a very much more interesting and refreshing person to be around. This narrow focus of attention takes us away from all the great information and events that are going on in the world and beyond.

People underestimate the power gained from reading, which can be priceless; reading expands your knowledge and awareness. Reading will also stimulate your creative imagination.

However, there is one negative aspect of reading, be careful when you read negative feedback because it can have a strong impact on your perceptions, beliefs, and what you do or do not achieve or attempt.

Reading can intrigue you while at the same time it will stir your imagination and unleash the creative part of your mind into action.

But as well as all the serious stuff, books can be fun too. Reading can take you back into history and days gone by; it can also give you an insight into the now, the future, and the still unknown and unsolved.

Reading is a Vocabulary Builder

I find it really hard to learn new arbitrary words at random and follow them. So, for me, a better and more interesting way of improving my vocabulary has been to read. Also, it helps me understand the various possible ways a word can be used and how.

Reading can help improve your vocabulary. Saying new words aloud helps you better recall them and pick them up, making these new words part of your daily vocabulary. Those with a higher vocabulary are considered more intelligent and are often taken more seriously in a work setting, opening up better career opportunities.

According to a paper from the University of California Berkeley, exposure to new vocabulary leads to higher scores on intelligence tests.

It's no secret that reading increases your vocabulary and improves your spelling, but did you know that reading increases your vocabulary more than talking or direct teaching? Reading forces us to look up words that we might not have seen or heard recently at the pub. In fact, language in children's books is likely to be more sophisticated than your average conversation.

Increased vocabulary is especially crucial for bloggers or writers. All successful writers will tell you that to write well, you need to read—every day. You'll be surprised at the words you start incorporating into your writing.

A beefier vocabulary isn't just for writers, though. Knowing what other people are saying and using the perfect words to convey your feelings is a critical part of being a better human. Better listeners are more successful in life.

You will come across many new phrases, words and eventually get accustomed to them. Hence you will have an improved vocabulary both in communication and writing.

How Reading Improves Languages

When reading, you might come across a few words you don't quite understand or even recognize. This confusion can lead you to look up the word and discover the definition. Both in book form or eBook form, dictionaries can be beneficial to your understanding of this new word you might not recognize. Because you didn't know the word to begin with, the act of searching for the definition helps your brain retain that new and exciting word. Consider how far your vocabulary has come since you first learned to read. You now know many new words that are more intelligent sounding than when you first started reading.

What does this do to benefit you? Well, after several days of reading and looking up new words you don't understand, your vocabulary will begin to expand one word at a time. When reading every day, words and phrases fill your brain with a new vocabulary that you might never have learned without reading. This is proven in this study by the University of Oregon.

Often, you might not even realize how much your vocabulary has increased after even just one day of heavy reading. These words that you have been learning will begin to integrate into your everyday vocabulary, and you will start to catch yourself using these words. It is incredible how much you take in while reading, and this aspect of understanding is another significant benefit of daily reading.

Reading Improves Writing

Good writing skills allow communicating your message with clarity, precision, and ease. One can reach a much larger audience through writing than through speaking. Writing skills thereby allow you to maintain clear communication and accurate documentation in any workplace. Writing does not require the sender or the receiver of the message to be at the same place or time. Writing skills allow you to communicate clearly with others and create useful resources for the workplace. Writing is a very important skill that should be practiced and acquired from an early age. By writing, you share your knowledge, your experience, and your views with millions of people.

Writing is the ability to express ideas through the written word. An organization needs employees with good writing abilities so that the opinions, thoughts, and ideas are communicated to the stakeholders properly and as intended; thereby, the ability to communicate ideas through writing is in high demand. Properly written documents, emails, and posts can have a high impact on the receiver's mind and persuade customers to purchase a product or convince investors to partner with a company. Good project documents, proposals, emails, technical documents, formatting of documents for different situations, etc., require good writing skills. The writing style and the tone based on the situation are important writing skills that matter.

Writing is one such skill that people wish to learn, but most do not succeed because they want quick success. Writing requires years of learning, practice, correcting, and improving. A good reader can learn quickly about writing. Writing comes with the flow, and flow comes with ideas. Writing means getting the idea, organizing it, and putting it on paper.

Besides good command of the language, writing requires a good understanding of the reader. Once you understand their requirements, you will be able to write effectively.

When you become a good writer, you earn respect, and people follow you. Hence writing skills are very important. Whether you are a student or an employee, writing skills help you in every field.

Reading Improves Writing

Reading improves writing without any doubt. The flow of writing appears when you read books regularly. It becomes easier to find the right words, ideas, and structure at the time of writing. Due to improvement in imagination, overall writing quality also improves very much. The students who develop the reading habit automatically become good writers later, distinguishing them from other fellow students. The more you read, the more you get the idea, more you improve your vocabulary and the language, thereby overall writing quality.

Those who write know the importance of reading. Whether you write things for work or just for fun, heavy reading can improve your writing skills and abilities. There are several ways in which reading can help strengthen your writing skills, and each of these ways happens without you even realizing it.

Reading and writing correlate positively; the more you read, the better your writing will be. I have experienced this firsthand. Musicians influence one another, and painters use techniques established by previous masters, so do writers learn by reading the works of others.

Writers are often big readers as well because they seek the fulfillment of reading. By concentrating on the way novels and other books are set up and written, you can mimic these styles, thus improving your writing skills considerably. Studying the writing of others is a great tool, especially if you enjoy writing. Even best-selling authors use this tool for studying writing styles and themes.

The best part about reading about how to improve your writing is there are various books written about the writing craft with information about all forms of writing. You can find these self-help books at any bookstore, both online and in-store. If you are a serious writer, you can read both novels and these amazing books on writing. Any form of reading can improve your writing tremendously.

What is the Co-relation?

Just as listening is related to speaking, reading is related to writing. The first important point to remember for improving writing is to read as much as you can. Reading improves vocabulary, grammar, sentence structure and shows different ways to communicate ideas. It also stimulates critical thinking on any subject. By reading, you get to know how these great writers use their words and write sentences. All these will help you develop your writing skills. When you study different types of writing and literature, you will understand the use of words, the flow of sentences, and how the author hooks the readers through his or her experiences.

The best writers are also keen readers, and regular reading is an easy way to develop your writing skills.

Expand your horizons to more challenging material than you typically read, and pay attention to sentence structure, word choice, and how the material flows.

Reading and Writing go hand in hand. One helps the other develop concepts and ideas and look into other people's minds and hearts.

Reading replenishes your thought processes, improves your vocabulary, increases your perspectives, and enhances your ability to manage language. Reading translations, in particular, gives you a multi-dimensional view of other writers.

Writers need to read a lot. Magazines. Books. Periodicals and so on. They need to grasp the art of language to appreciate the finer points of words. As they read, they should jot down ideas and capture thoughts as they come. As a writer, you'll find yourself hitting plateaus and roadblocks when you aren't reading. You'll run out of words if you're not regularly being challenged through books and other material.

Lots of these new and invigorating thoughts embed in your mind, and you get better at your writing. To get even better, expand your reading into as many genres as you can manage. You may be surprised to know your writing will tangentially expand too. The need to stay writing in a confined territory slowly vanishes, and your ability to work in different themes and tones comes from close reading.

When it is time to write, you will not go looking for ways to write whatever you want to write. You have run the hard yards and enjoyed it all along.

If your writing is just is not up to the mark, the reader will realize it even if he is not an academician or grammar god. People can easily recognize bad writing. Don't read to accomplish anything. You don't need to read to finish what you're reading. Just read to read. Make reading a habit, a personal passion.

As a writer, words are your lifeblood. Read anything. Just get started. Reading can improve your writing skills because it will add new words to your dictionary. The more you read, the newer words you'll get, which you can use in your writings. When you start writing anything on topics, you can use new words which you have learned. Whenever you read new books, you understand the meaning, but besides that, you also analyze the way of writing, which helps you write properly.

Reading Reduces Stress

Many things in life can lead to stress. The loss of a job, debt and financial issues, family problems, failures, relationship issues, and demanding jobs are the causes of stress. Even positive life changes, such as moving to a bigger house, getting a job promotion, or going on holiday, can be sources of stress.

All of us can relate to at least a few of the feelings described above and felt stressed and overwhelmed at some point in time. Some people seem to be more affected by stress than others. For some people, leaving the house on time each morning can be a very stressful experience. At the same time, others may be able to cope with a great deal of pressure.

When you are stressed, you may experience many different feelings, including anxiety, fear, anger, sadness, or frustration. Managing stress is challenging to many persons, particularly for those who are not so mentally stronger. In case of any setback, their negative emotions take over and control the mind in the direction of a negative impact and its consequences resulting in stressful mental health.

Stress can affect many parts of your daily life, and after long periods of intense stress, it can even be harmful to your overall health. Reading both novels and other literature can help solve the issues that stress causes by allowing your mind and body to relax. Once you start reading, you will start to focus on your stress and the words and storyline. In time, reading will lower your stress level, making you feel better mentally and physically.

Reading Helps to De-stress

One of the fascinating benefits of reading is that it helps to reduce stress significantly. Many of us are exhausted in our busy and hectic lives, and we are always looking for ways to deal with these anxieties. Well, believe it or not, reading can actually help you de-stress. No matter how much stress you had at work or in your personal relationships or countless other issues faced in daily life, it all just slips away when you get involved in reading a good book. Reading is the best way to relax your brain. As per the Research Psychologist, the human mind has to concentrate on reading, and the distraction of being taken into a literary world eases the tensions in muscles and the heart.

Reading enables you to relax and de-stress your mind and help pull you into a deep and peaceful sleep. Books are a great company at night. Choose a good book before going to bed and relax your mind yourself. A book can put you in a good mood and relaxes your mind and soul. At the end of a hectic, stressful day, you need a good book to keep you peaceful and stress-free.

Sometimes, there is no need to spend lots of money on professionals and programs to achieve a sense of calm when a simple book can solve everything. Reading is the ideal way to relax and calm those anxious nerves that are constantly at work.

You read that little fact right, though it seems strange to say. The act of reading and focusing on the written word can help relieve your mind of anxiety and the pressures of the day. By pulling your mind away from the stress at hand, you can relax and let the stress melt away.

Reading sounds almost too good to be true, but how does reading decrease stress? While reading, your brain immediately transports itself to a different world with different people. This change in pace can be a breath of fresh air for someone who is stressed out or suffers from extended periods of stress. By reading, you can allow yourself to take a breath, relax, and be swept away to another world through the words written on the page.

Books can bring joy to your life daily. The act of reading is a great benefit both to mental and physical health, but it can also brighten your day. Sometimes, the days can be stressful and worrisome, but when you lay down at night and curl up with a good book, it lifts your spirits along with that stress and worry.

There's no reason to feel upset about stressful situations. Just take some time out of your day, read a little bit, and feel yourself relaxing. As compelling as meditation and yoga are at brightening your day, a little time spent alone with a book is a lovely way to spend your afternoon or night. Books are easy to carry around, especially with the popular e-readers, and you can enjoy your reading time anywhere.

From vacations to a quick moment while waiting in the carpool line, reading is an effective means of relaxation in an otherwise busy world. If you love to get up early, you should start your day with a little light reading. Your day will be just a little bit brighter, and you can breathe easily. Let books take a little weight off your shoulders so you can enjoy the things around you. Take a few moments for yourself and just read.

When you read, it reduces your stress by taking your focus of attention off your worries. The mental activity you receive that acts like a workout for the mind are believed to help slow down or prevent the onset of dementia.

Secondly, if you read regularly, it can help you relax and quieten your mind, which can help you reduce your stress levels.

Reading helps in reducing stress. It helps you to disengage yourself from the real world and dive into a new creative one. Recent studies have proven that reading helps to put our brain into a pleasurable state- like a state similar to meditation. It brings the same health benefits of deep relaxation and inner calmness.

Reading is the best medicine for your stress. Like everyone, I've been through times very depressing and very hard, times when I lost myself when I felt that I had no one by my side, times when I could not say to anyone what I went through, times when I gave up on everything, times when things shattered, times when everything seemed to be fake, times when I felt the end of all. But, to my rescue, I had those books. The only thing that made me comfortable and helped me get through all of this was reading books. I seriously am indebted to the books for being my strength and support.

Reading has always been my only way to get rid of my stress. It takes me to a different, beautiful world, and I absolutely love it. Reading engages the brain and has a positive effect on the brain.

How To Improve Reading

"There is a great deal of difference between an eager man who wants to read a book and the tired man who wants a book to read."–Gilbert K. Chesterton

I have faced lots of twists and turns in my life, particularly for reading. My reading journey has been off and on throughout my life. I remember after my tenth and twelfth examinations, I read a book daily. Reading continued, although not regularly, and that helped me to know a lot. I have never been a bookworm except for short periods of life. But I have been a regular reader. When reading becomes a passion, definitely you can make reading a regular habit. But where passion is lacking, it needs some effort to make reading a habit. I personally believe that the following tips can be very helpful for developing the habit of reading. Although some may or may not apply to individuals, it is better to pick up the ones which suit you.

1. **Read the book similar to your interests**: This is the most important point to keep in mind. Randomly picking up a novel will not help. Find the genre you like; it may be fiction, non-fiction, mystery, self-help, romance, etc. Analyze your interest in the books, choose a good genre and start reading. If you enjoy reading, you won't feel a burden. Start with short novels and then move on to big ones. Reading shorter books might be advisable as you get started. The goal here is to finish the books. Finishing a book acts as a motivator for reading another book.

2. **Find Time:** If you really want to read more, try reducing TV, use of smartphones, or the Internet. This

may be difficult for many people. Still, every minute you spend away from the Internet/TV, you could use it for reading. This could create hours of book reading time.

3. **Visit book store and book fair**: If you do not know where to start or do not feel like reading at home, you should visit the bookstore in your locality and just spend some time out there, and I am sure you will find something that interests you. These places are so cool to hang out. Visiting a book fair will also help.

4. **Avail library membership:** A great way to squeeze more reading into your hectic life is to surround yourself with books. You can be a member of a library. Libraries are very much cheaper, and you get to spend some time reading in a supportive environment. In the beginning, you may get

disheartened when you have to spend money on books, so better get a library card and borrow books. When you visit the library regularly, you automatically get the motivation to read.

5. **Set the time**: You make a schedule of reading daily or set a particular time according to the time availability. Remember to adhere to it no matter what strictly. In short, give reading a priority rather than doing it as a task and making it a part of a living.

6. **Carry a book in your bag**: Wherever you go, carry the book with you. For example, you can utilize that time in reading books if you commute daily by bus or train. Whenever you visit someplace or meet somebody, you may need to wait for any reason, rather than idly wasting time you can read a book. It

is much more productive than using your smartphone.

7. **Make a list of the books**: You list all the good books you want to read and keep updating that list periodically. The list will help you to motivate for reading those books.

8. **Keep a record**. You should record the title and author of the books you read, along with the dates you start and finish them. At the end of the book, write a note on your thoughts about the book. It is extremely satisfying to look back after some time to see all the great books you have read. It can be encouraging when you look at the number of books you have read. Even note down whatever you have learned from a particular book, which can be useful for you for your whole life, and it can help you find a solution to

whatever problem you will be going through.

9. **Start reading one author:** Reading the same author actually gives the advantage of knowing that author's voice- tone and the distinctive writing style, and it is much easier to finish a book.

"To acquire the habit of reading is to construct for yourself a refuge from almost all the miseries of life." — W. Somerset Maugham

Reading is one of the best qualities that an individual should have. Books are often known to be your best friend for a specific reason. So, it is essential to build a good reading habit within oneself. We must all read daily for at least 30 minutes to enjoy the knowledge gained from reading. It gives a reader great pleasure to sit in a quiet place and enjoy reading without any disturbance. Reading books as a hobby is the most enjoyable experience a person can have. Books contain vast amounts of information which can only be learned by reading them. So, it is very important to develop a good reading habit.

Reading is a very good habit that one needs to develop in the course of life. Good books can inform you, enlighten you, and reading them will lead you in the right direction. There cannot be a better companion than a good book.

Reading is beneficial because it is suitable for your overall development. Once you start reading, you experience and imagine a whole new scenario in your mind. When a person starts loving the habit of reading, they will eventually get addicted to it. Reading helps you to develop your language skills and vocabulary. Reading books is also a way in which people can relax and reduce stress. It is beneficial to read a good book for a few minutes to expand the brain muscles for healthy functioning and better memory power.

Reading is one of the best habits one can have because it improves your imagination and offers you a vast amount of knowledge. Books are your best friend or your best companion as reading helps you build up your confidence and uplift your mood. Reading can help you grow mentally and give you a new perspective about everything in life. Good books can positively influence people and guide you in the right direction in life. The more you engage yourself in reading, the more you fall in love with it. Reading helps you to enhance your language skills and vocabulary. Reading will help you relax and reduce stress.

Reading improves your creativity and enhances your understanding of life in a better way. Reading also inspires you to write, and by doing that, one will surely fall in love with writing. If you want to adopt some good habits in life, then reading should be on the top of your list as it plays a vital role in the overall growth and development of a person. You can say that reading can change your life for the better, and the importance of reading is undeniable. If you think that you hate reading books, then perhaps you just have yet to find the genre for your own personal style

— but keep trying and keep searching for what's right for you. A book is one of the most powerful things in the world, offering you new opportunities to learn, grow, and be inspired!

Books are amazing things that can be both entertaining and beneficial to your health. They are almost like tools for a healthy lifestyle. Those who read daily understand the importance of a good book. The books that you choose to read can range from romance to non-fiction. Often, people will read magazine articles or even textbooks if that is what they enjoy reading. Whatever you choose to read, you get multiple benefits of reading to help your mind and body.

Voracious readers will always have a book in their hands as well. As a reader, you probably don't think of the great benefits of reading either, but they are there even when you don't realize it. From stress relief to improved memory, reading is hugely beneficial in all aspects of our lives. Reading is a great way to improve yourself all around.

You can find books anywhere, from the library to bookstores to thrift shops. The options of books or magazines to read are limitless. The kind of books you enjoy reading is as simple as trying out a few genres. If you prefer real stories, go with non-fiction. If you prefer mystical stories of fantasy, romance, etc., then give fiction a chance.

If you are not an avid reader, give it a good try. Initially, you may feel bored, but with a little time, you will start loving it. Just follow the methods of how to improve reading mentioned in the previous chapter. With all of the amazing benefits of reading, everybody should try to develop this habit.

*****

Disclaimer

Although the publisher and the author have made every effort to ensure that the information in this book is correct, and while this publication is designed to provide accurate information regarding the subject matter covered, the publisher and the author assume no responsibility for errors, inaccuracies, omissions, or any other inconsistencies herein and hereby disclaim any liability to any party for any loss, damage, or disruption caused by errors or omissions, and whether such errors or omissions result from negligence, accident, or any other cause.

The ideas, procedures, and suggestions in this book are not intended as a substitute for consulting with an expert. Neither the author nor the publisher shall be liable or responsible for any loss or damage allegedly arising from any information or suggestion in this book.

Names, characters, and incidents in this book are either the product of the author's imagination or used in a fictitious manner. Any resemblance to an actual person, living or dead, or actual events is purely coincidental.